# TIME FOR KIDS READERS

## Election

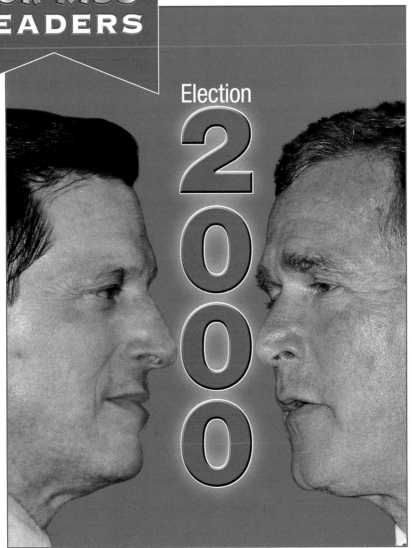

# 2000

by Elaine Israel

# Harcourt

Orlando   Austin   Chicago   New York   Toronto   London   San Diego

Visit *The Learning Site!*
**www.harcourtschool.com**

After a hard-fought election, George W. Bush was sworn in as the 43rd President.

George W. Bush became the new President of the United States on January 20, 2001. The weather in Washington, D.C., that Inauguration Day was rainy and cold, but this was a celebration that neither drizzle nor snow could stop. After all, it followed what was called "the wildest election in history."

Here's what usually happens during a presidential election: Every four years, on the first Tuesday after the first Monday in November, Americans vote to choose their leader. Before people vote, the candidates campaign for 18 months. During that time, candidates must first get their political party's nominations by winning state primary elections. Then, the parties choose their candidates. Afterwards, the campaigns pick up speed. No two presidential campaigns have been alike. Some have had surprises, none more so than the election of 2000. To understand this election, it's important to know how the electoral college works.

Election Extra ★
NEW YORK POST 25 CENTS
ELECTION EXTRA www.nypost.com

BUSH WINS

Austin American-Statesman

Bush!
Florida seals it: Texan elected 43rd president

3

# The Electoral College Is Not a

Q: Do people graduate from the electoral college?
A: The electoral college is not a school. It is actually a group of people, but this is just not just any group. This group chooses the President of the United States.

Q: How is the number of electors in the electoral college decided for each state?
A: The number of electors is equal to the total number of senators and representatives a state has in Congress.

Q: So, that makes how many electors?
A: 538. The District of Columbia gets three.

Q: Can electors vote for whomever they want?

A: The candidate that got the most votes in a state is supposed to win all the electoral votes for that state. Twenty-six states require electors to vote with the popular vote. However, nineteen states and the District of Columbia have no requirements that electors vote the way the popular vote in their state went. They don't punish electors who go their own way. Only five states do that, but the fines are small.

Q: Where do the electors meet?
A: They usually meet in their state capitals on the first Monday after the second Wednesday in December after the election.

Q: What happens then?
A: The electoral votes are officially counted during a special session of Congress.

# School

Q: What happens if no candidate gets a majority of electoral votes?
A: The vote goes to the House of Representatives. It chooses among the three candidates who received the most electoral votes. But— wait! Individual members don't cast ballots. Each state gets one vote. That's when little Rhode Island has as much power as big California.

Q: Then who chooses the Vice President?
A: Individuals in the Senate must choose from the two vice-presidential candidates who received the most vice-presidential votes in the electoral college.

Electors usually meet to vote in state capitols, such as this one in Nashville, Tennessee.

# Want to know more?

## HERE ARE THREE FACTS ABOUT THE ELECTORAL COLLEGE.

**1.** The electoral college was a last-minute addition to the U.S. Constitution. Some of its writers disagreed over how the President and Vice President should be chosen. Some wanted Congress to pick the President. Others wanted the citizens to choose directly. Some didn't think that ordinary people were smart enough to choose their own leader. The electoral college was a compromise.

**2.** Because of the electoral college system, the President and Vice President are the nation's only two elected officials who aren't elected directly by the people.

**3.** The electoral college may result in a new President who didn't win the popular vote. That happened in the elections of 1824, 1876, 1888, and in 2000. In 1888, according to historians, Grover Cleveland won the popular vote. Benjamin Harrison, though, became President by winning the electoral college vote.

In 1888 Grover Cleveland (left) won the popular vote over Benjamin Harrison. However, Harrison became President by winning more votes in the electoral college.

And Now

Gore and Bush supporters show their views in Tallahassee, Florida.

# The Wildest Election in History...

**Election Day, November 7, 2000** The Republican candidate was Texas Governor George W. Bush. The Democratic candidate was U.S. Vice President Al Gore. Among the candidates from smaller parties, called third parties, were Ralph Nader and Pat Buchanan.

More than one hundred and one million voters from all over the United States went to the polls. Around the world, people would watch the results come in on television. The next day, as after past elections, it was assumed that life would more or less return to normal.

Early that morning, something already seemed wrong. Joan Joseph, a Democratic party official in Palm Beach County, Florida, reported to Gore headquarters that there was a problem with the ballots. She said, "The ballots do not line up. . . . People who think they are voting for Gore could be voting for Pat Buchanan, because the word Democrat is lined up with [the name] Buchanan."

**7:50 P.M.** The results started to trickle in. The TV anchors began announcing which candidate had won each state. The networks agreed that Al Gore had won Florida. Soon other states lined up in Gore's column. It seemed as if Bush had lost.

Then Ed Gillespie, who worked for the Bush campaign, called the networks. He argued that the outcome in Florida was too close to call. He was angry that the anchors had reported that Gore had won.

The networks didn't change their reports. They relied on information provided by a company called Voter News Service. Its workers question people who have just voted. "Who did you vote for?" they ask. This is called an *exit poll* and it's usually dependable. But everyone was in for a huge shock. For the first time since the exit polls had been in use, some of the numbers—reported from parts of Florida—were inaccurate.

**9:55 P.M.** The TV networks, starting with CNN, began reporting that Florida was too close to call.

**1:30 A.M.** Both major candidates now had 242 electoral college votes. To win, a candidate needs 270 electoral votes. Florida's 25 electoral votes became essential for winning the election.

PALM BEACH COUNTY, FLORIDA
NOVEMBER 7, 2000

GENERAL ELECTION
COUNTY, FLORIDA
BER 7, 2000

| (REPUBLICAN) | 3▸▸ | | (REFORM) |
| GE W. BUSH · PRESIDENT | | | PAT BUCHANAN · PRESIDENT |
| CHENEY · VICE PRESIDENT | | ◂◂ 4 | EZOLA FOSTER · VICE PRESIDENT |
| (DEMOCRATIC) | 5▸▸ | | (SOCIALIST) |
| ORE · PRESIDENT | | | DAVID McREYNOLDS · PRESIDENT |
| LIEBERMAN · VICE PRESIDENT | | ◂◂ 6 | MARY CAL HOLLIS · VICE PRESIDENT |
| (LIBERTARIAN) | 7▸▸ | | (CONSTITUTION) |
| RRY BROWNE · PRESIDENT | | | HOWARD PHILLIPS · PRESIDENT |
| T OLIVIER · VICE PRESIDENT | | ◂◂ 8 | J. CURTIS FRAZIER · VICE PRESIDENT |
| (GREEN) | 9▸▸ | | (WORKERS WORLD) |
| ALPH NADER · PRESIDENT | | | MONICA MOOREHEAD · PRESIDENT |
| INONA LaDUKE · VICE PRESIDENT | | ◂◂ 10 | GLORIA La RIVA · VICE PRESIDENT |
| (SOCIALIST WORKERS) | 11▸▸ | | WRITE-IN CANDIDATE |
| AMES HARRIS · PRESIDENT | | | To vote for a write-in candidate, follow the |
| MARGARET TROWE · VICE PRESIDENT | | | directions on the long stub of your ballot card. |
| (NATURAL LAW) | 13▸▸ | | |
| JOHN HAGELIN · PRESIDENT | | | |
| NAT GOLDHABER · VICE PRESIDENT | | | |

Approximately 206 million people were qualified to vote in the 2000 election. Less than one-half that number of people cast a vote.

The voting system used in Palm Beach County, Florida, confused some voters.

**2:15 A.M.** The networks gave Florida's 25 electoral votes to Bush. One after the other, the exhausted television news anchors declared that George W. Bush was the new president. In Austin, Texas, the Bush family was relieved and excited. They got ready to celebrate.

In Nashville, Tennessee, as his daughters cried, Al Gore began to write his concession speech, saying he had lost.

**2:30 A.M.** Gore called Bush to concede. "You're a good man," Bush told his rival.

Al Gore, his family, and his supporters—all tired and discouraged—headed for the local war memorial. There, in the rainy night, he would give his concession speech.

But in Florida, the Board of Elections declared that the difference of votes between Bush and Gore had dropped to 200. Florida law says that such a narrow margin means there must be a recount.

**3:45 A.M.** Gore made another phone call to Bush. "As you may have noticed," said Gore, "things have changed."

Gore told Bush that because of the closeness of the vote in Florida he could not concede the election after all. Both candidates anxiously awaited news from Florida.

**6:15 A.M.** The American people awoke to hear a real surprise. It was the day after Election Day, and the nation had no President-elect! No one had been chosen to succeed the current President.

# How

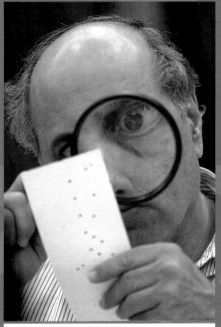

An election official in Florida looks over a disputed punch card ballot.

Some voters go into voting machines and pull levers. Other voters punch cards. Still others use touch screens, push buttons, or even submit handwritten ballots. Our nation has a variety of voting methods. That's because the U.S. Constitution allows each state to decide how its citizens will vote. Most states leave the method up to individual cities and counties.

# Voters vote

**BALLOT: Touch Screen**

**BALLOT: Lever**

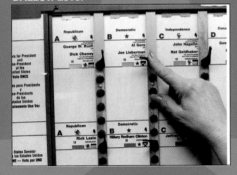

**BALLOT: Punch Card**

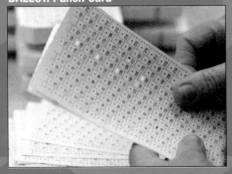

## A Mess of Ballots

Few people gave ballots much thought until Election 2000. Thirty-four percent of voters–more than three out of 10–used punch cards in the 2000 election. These voters were given cards on which they had to punch a hole opposite their choice. Computers then read the ballots. The problem was that sometimes the holes were not completely punched, leaving little pieces of paper hanging from them.
The computers had trouble reading these cards, so it was possible those votes were not counted.

On some "butterfly" ballots, the name of the party did not line up with the name of the candidate. That's what Joan Joseph had noticed in Florida. That's how Pat Buchanan received more than 3,000 votes from people even he admitted would never have chosen him. Oddly enough, the ballot was approved because its large type was supposed to be easier to read by Florida's older residents.

In New Mexico, 500 paper ballots were incorrectly recorded. The handwriting on them couldn't be read! In fact, 2 percent of all ballots in modern-day Presidential elections are not counted, partly because of errors by voters.

The Florida Supreme Court met to decide if election ballots should be recounted in Florida.

Some votes in Florida needed to be counted again. And so they were, slowly and by hand. The method of recounting was challenged several times. The recount started, stopped, and started again. The recount stopped again. Then ballots from people living overseas came in. Arguments about them arose. Lawyers for both Bush and Gore went to state courts and federal courts. Watching the news from Florida became a lot like watching a Ping-Pong game. Ping! The ball was in Bush's favor. Pong! The ball was in Gore's favor.

Florida wasn't the only state with a very close vote. In Wisconsin, the difference between Bush and Gore was fewer than 6,000 votes. The Vice President lost his home state, Tennessee, by a narrow margin.

In this map of Florida, blue blocks are counties that voted for Bush, red blocks are counties for Gore.

No one can ever claim that his or her vote doesn't count. In this election, a lot of people must have felt that way.

**Five weeks after the election** Looming over the undecided election was the date of December 12. That is the day when all 50 states must cast their electoral votes.

Finally, the case went to the highest court in the land, the U.S. Supreme Court. It has nine justices whose job it is to decide whether a law or an action violates the U.S. Constitution. The court ruled that the extended hand recount in Florida was unlawful. The court also said that there was not enough time to have another recount that would be in keeping with the deadlines set by the Constitution.

The counting was stopped. The Supreme Court, by a vote of five to four, supported the arguments made by lawyers for George W. Bush. He would become the 43rd President of the United States.

**December 13, 2000** Al Gore, saying he disagreed with the court, conceded the election. "I'm with you, Mr. President," said Gore. "And God bless you."

**January 20, 2001** After being sworn in as President, George W. Bush delivered his inauguration speech. He began the speech by pointing out that in the United States peaceful elections are one of the things that make our country special. Bush said, "The peaceful transfer of authority is rare in history, yet common in our country. With a simple oath, we affirm old traditions and make new beginnings." Bush also recognized his election opponent, saying, "I thank Vice President Gore for a contest conducted with spirit and ended with grace."

Protesters demonstrated outside the Supreme Court while the justices decided whether to allow a recount.

# How the States Voted

Bush won nearly every southern state. Gore won several big electoral states such as California, Pennsylvania, New York, and Illinois.

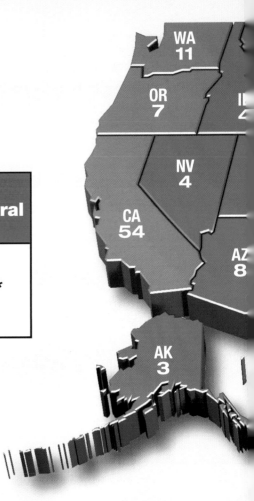

| The Candidates | The Popular Vote | The Electoral Vote |
|---|---|---|
| Gore | 50,992,335 | 266 |
| Bush | 50,455,156 | 271* |
| Nader | 2,882,897 | 0 |

Source: Information Please Almanac
*There is a total of 538 electoral votes. One elector from the District of Columbia did not vote.

## About George W. Bush

George W. Bush was born into a powerful family. His grandfather Prescott Bush was a U.S. senator. His father, George Bush, was U.S. President from 1989 to 1993. But George W. insists that following in his father's footsteps was never his goal. "I didn't have this life plan," he told TIME magazine. "I didn't know what I wanted to be, and I tried a variety of different things, like working in the oil industry, in campaigns, in a poverty program."

George W. was born in New Haven, Connecticut, in 1946. When he was two, his family moved to Texas, where he attended public school. At 15, he returned to the East to attend private school in Massachusetts.

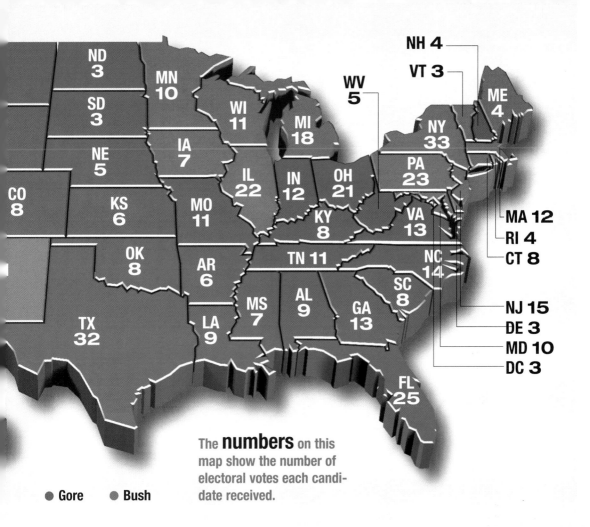

ND 3
MN 10
SD 3
WI 11
MI 18
WV 5
NH 4
VT 3
ME 4
NE 5
IA 7
NY 33
PA 23
CO 8
IL 22
IN 12
OH 21
KS 6
MO 11
KY 8
VA 13
MA 12
RI 4
CT 8
OK 8
AR 6
TN 11
NC 14
SC 8
NJ 15
DE 3
MD 10
DC 3
TX 32
MS 7
AL 9
GA 13
LA 9
FL 25

The **numbers** on this map show the number of electoral votes each candidate received.

● Gore    ● Bush

Bush says his mom largely shaped his character. Barbara Bush taught her son to speak his mind. "Dad gives me advice when I ask him for it, my mom when I don't. She can be blunt like me," says Bush.

Bush admits that he was blessed with many advantages. He says that he "inherited a good name, but you don't inherit a vote. You have to win a vote."

George W. is married to Laura, a former teacher. They have twin daughters, Barbara and Jenna, who are college students.

Jeb Bush, another son of former President George Bush, was elected governor of Florida in 1998, the same year George W. was reelected governor of Texas. They are only the second set of brothers ever to serve as state governors at the same time. The others were Nelson and Winthrop Rockefeller of New York and Arkansas, who served from 1967 to 1971.

15

# A Few of George W. Bush's Favorites

| KID'S BOOK | CHILDHOOD HERO | MUSICIANS |
|---|---|---|

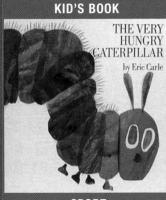

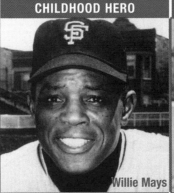

Willie Mays

The Everly Brothers

| SPORT | SNACK | COLOR |
|---|---|---|

blue

FAST FACTS

- John Quincy Adams lost both the electoral college and the popular vote in 1824 but still became President. He was elected by the House of Representatives.
- The 2000 presidential election was one of the closest popular votes in history. The closest was in 1960. John F. Kennedy defeated Richard Nixon by only 118,574 votes.
- The candidate with the largest electoral vote was Ronald Reagan. In 1984 he won 525 electoral votes. In that year, he also carried the most states—49. He shares that record with Richard Nixon, who also won 49 states in 1972.
- The longest inaugural speech was delivered by William Henry Harrison in 1841. It was 8,445 words and lasted for one hour and 45 minutes.

## Think and Respond

①  What U.S. state played a deciding role in the 2000 election?

②  Explain the electoral college and how it works.

③  Name the four ballot techniques that people use to vote. What problems arose from some of the ballots during the 2000 election?

④  Describe the final outcome of the 2000 election.

⑤  Would you like to run for an elected office? Explain your answer.

**Design a Ballot** Ballots and their design played a big role in the 2000 election. Design a ballot that would be easy for voters to use and to tally. Share your design with the class.

## HARCOURT HORIZONS

UNITED STATES HISTORY: BEGINNINGS
UNITED STATES HISTORY

# Harcourt

www.harcourtschool.com

ISBN 0-15-333595-5

90000>

9 780153 335952

TIME
FOR KIDS
READERS

# Canada's
## French Province

Harcourt

by Nanette Kalis

*Photo Credits*

Cover ©Ray Juno/Corbis Stock Market; P.2-3 ©J. A. Kraulis/Masterfile; P.4 ©North Wind Pictures; P.5 ©North Wind Pictures; P.6 top by PhotoDisc; P.6 bottom ©North Wind Pictures; P.7 ©Culver Pictures; P.8 ©North Wind Pictures; P.9 Courtesy of Nelson.com; P.11 top ©J. A. Kraulis/Masterfile; P.11 bottom Courtesy of Quebec Historical Society; P.12-13 ©Granger Collection; P.15 ©Hulton Archive/Getty Images; P.17 ©Hulton Archive/Getty Images; P.18 ©Joe Viesti/Viesti Associates; P.19 ©Walter Bibikow/Viesti Associates; P.20-21 ©Winston Fraser; P.20 inset ©Jose Azel/Aurora/PictureQuest ; P.23 left ©Connie Coleman/Getty Images; P.23 right ©Walter Bibikow/Viesti Associates; P.24 ©Winston Fraser

*Book Design*

Art Director: Barbara Love Ong-Shen
Designers: Laurie Murphy, Colleen Pidel, Sufjan Stevens, Jacqueline L. Kelly and William Kelly

Printed in Mexico

ISBN 0-15-333557-2

Ordering Options
ISBN 0-15-333547-5      Grade 5 Collection
ISBN 0-15-333558-0      Grade 5, Book 5, Package of 5

6 7 8 9 10   126   10 09 08 07 06 05

# TIME
## FOR KIDS
# READERS

# Canada's
## *French Province*

by Nanette Kalis

# Harcourt

Orlando   Austin   Chicago   New York   Toronto   London   San Diego

Visit *The Learning Site!*
www.harcourtschool.com

Quebec is almost three times as large as France, and much of this huge province is forest land.